Poetry by street-connected young people globally

Compiled by Samantha Richards

In collaboration with Street Child United

First published February 2021 by Fly on the Wall Press

Published in the UK by

Fly on the Wall Press

56 High Lea Rd

New Mills

Derbyshire

SK22 3DP

www.flyonthewallpoetry.co.uk

ISBN: 978-1-913211-20-2

The right of the individual poets to be identified as the authors of their work has been asserted in accordance with the Copyright, Designs and Patents Act 1988. The right of Isabelle Kenyon to be identified as the editor of this work has been asserted in accordance with the Copyright, Designs and Patents Act 1988.

Typesetting and Cover Design by Isabelle Kenyon. Street Child United Photography courtesy of Wilf Whitty, Malachy McCrudden, Kylie Milne, WBR Photo Gustavo Oliveira, Chris Cellier, Rebecca Morton, Stanislav Borisov, Polina Bykona, Paul Fontanelli, Leseya Guseva, Elena Kuznetsova, Ilya Maliy, Kristina Mikhailyk, Vicky Roy, Angelina Vovk, Tim Vyner, Rosie Hallam, Mary Humphrey, Alex Kirschtein, Madeleine Waller.

All rights reserved. No part of this publication may be reproduced, stored in or introduced into a retrieval system, or transmitted in any form, or by any means (electronic, mechanical, photocopying, recording or otherwise) without prior written permissions of the publisher. Any person who does any unauthorised act in relation to this publication may be liable for criminal prosecution and civil claims for damages.

A CIP Catalogue record for this book is available from the British Library.

A Letter from Street Child United Young Leader, Samantha Richards

(On her experience of working with the charity and on compiling the work within this anthology):

In 2018 I had the honour of being chosen to represent my country at the Street Child World Cup, Moscow. I was overwhelmed when my coach, Jack, called me, explaining that I would be flown out to Russia to participate in the tournament. The Street Child World Cup wasn't just a football tournament – it meant so much more than that – but it was a long road to get there.

I left school after my GCSEs thinking that education wasn't for me. Fortunately, I was selected to study with Arsenal FC on a programme where I would coach and play football whilst working towards a BTEC Level 3 in Sport.

Arsenal identified me as a vulnerable young person, at risk of going down the wrong path. They introduced me to Centrepoint, a youth homelessness charity, and I began to take part in their weekly women's football sessions.

Week by week my confidence grew, and I was starting to talk about the problems that I was facing at the time. Whether it was to do with my struggles with mental health, being bullied or my grandad attempting to take his own life, Centrepoint helped me channel my emotions and enhance my coping skills, as well as developing me as a footballer and coach.

I was chosen for Centrepoint's Team England football programme – this meant that I would have training camps at St George's Park, where the Lionesses train, as well as having the possibility of being chosen to compete at an international event. To say that I was ecstatic was an understatement. I had begun to see my own potential, and started to achieve more and more in life: I got my first job and I was doing well with my BTEC, which enabled me to channel my energy into my passion for coaching.

My coaches must also have seen the progress I was making because, with my nine teammates, I was selected for the Street Child World Cup, and in May 2018 we were on our way to Moscow.

I wasn't prepared for the emotional side of the tournament. I was captivated by the stories of the street-connected children from all around the world. The passion and determination in their voices when talking about the challenges they had faced was something that would stay with me forever. The tournament was made up of three parts: football, congress and the arts. For me, it was no longer about football abilities, it was about the struggles that we face in our communities back at home and dealing with the stereotypes at-risk young people face.

In congress, Team England were paired with Team India and we learned a lot about our new friends' backgrounds. The girls that I shared a football pitch with that morning now told us their stories – stories of young women being snatched from their parents and trafficked, of girls forced into child marriage, of not legally existing because of not being registered at birth - and I was in the bathroom in tears because of it.

Having shared such a profound experience with my new friends, I wanted to help them. I wanted to help others like them, and others like me.

When I returned to the UK, I wasn't sure how to deal with all my emotions until I found a pen and paper. I began to write down words every day about how I was feeling; some days it would be happy, some days it would be sad and some days it would even be angry.

I started to put together a poem from what I wrote, to say thank you to Street Child United for allowing me and my friends from all around the world to have this life-changing opportunity. I wrote about my emotions and spoke of our needs as vulnerable young people.

I realised how powerful poetry can be. It can instil hope, it can inspire and you can feel the emotion in the words.

I thought to myself: writing, drawing or being creative, could help my new friends and others release their emotions like I had. What if I collected their poems and drawings in a book, bringing together the voices of young people from across the world? What if I could create a book which could be a voice filled with hope and truth?

From that idea came this book of poetry and artwork, a creative platform for people across the world to speak safely and have their voices heard. I hope you enjoy the work, and if you are facing your own challenges, remember:
We Are All Somebody.

John Wroe, BEM
Founder and CEO, Street Child United:

The Street Child World Cup is more than a game. It is only possible because the whole world conspires with us.

Andile, a young man who played for South Africa at the very first Street Child World Cup in 2010, said: *"When people see us by the streets, they say that we are street boys. But when they see us playing football, they say that we are not the street boys – they say that we are people like them."* Sport is a leveller unlike any other, connecting people in ways that only sport can. The Street Child World Cup exists to create a global platform for amazing young people like Andile, and the organisations who support them, so their voices are heard across the world.

We see the young people who take part in Street Child World Cups go on to achieve things that continue to amaze and inspire us, and this book is testament to that. Not only has Samantha had the courage and strength to drive her dream from ambition to reality, but she has given so many other young people the opportunity to stay connected and to be a continued part of something important. Her book contains messages of sadness and despair, but there are also messages of great resilience, power and determination and these are the messages that we often hear being shouted loudest at Street Child World Cups. These young people are the most inspiring young people you are ever likely to meet and by reading Samantha's book today, you are helping to ensure that their voices continue to be heard.

So, whether you are life-long member of the Street Child United family, or are joining us for the very first time today, take motivation from the poetry you are about to read. Listen to our young people and use these messages to inspire you every day.

To Samantha – the biggest thank you. You are somebody.

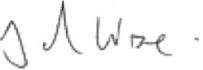

Contents

Young Leader Profiles	9
We Are Somebody By Samantha Richards	32
Unique By Agnes	33
We Are All One By Karina	34
I Live In a World By Jamilet	35
Battle Scars of the Drug War By Ronalyn (Bi-lingual)	38
Respond By Manty	40
Artwork by Manoj More	41
We Are All Family By Samantha Richards	48
I May Be By Abdallah	49
Rise By Sadock	50
Why? By Safiyyah	52
A Girl By Nisha	53
We Are United By Farijal	54
Hello, COVID-19 By Razib	55
Speak the truth By Aman Bharti	56
Soul of the Street By Taofeek	57
From the streets, to home By Ugochukw	59
COVID-19 By Mohammed Koroma	61
Hope for the future By Opeyemi	62
Street Trouble By Jimoh	63
Artwork By Thamizharasi	65
Coronavirus in the Streets By Ange (Bi-lingual)	66
The Story of a Street Child By Gladys	68

Precautions By Sheku	70
Implications By Alhaji	71
Destruction By Amanita	72
COVID-19, We Shall Threaten You By Amadu	73
Corona, Return To Your Harbour By Margret	74
A Tale of the Sitting Room By Musa, Juma, Rafeal, Gasta, Muzafaru, Paul, Omal, Mohammed, Shafik, Charles, Yasini, Owen, Ashraf, Alpha, Yusuf, Moses, Harunah, Bakali, Mutwalibi, Peter, Yasini, Brian, and Phillip	76
Is It Right? By Tamizharasi	78
Thank You By Samantha Richards	79

We Are Somebody

TEAM BANGLADESH

"When we came to the Street Child Cricket World Cup, we learned why it is so important to have a legal identity. We need to be able to prove that we are citizens of Bangladesh so that we have rights and dignity. Without a legal identity, I have no rights as a citizen of Bangladesh. We call on the government to create laws to provide a legal identity for all street children; to stop engagement of all children under 18 in any form of labour, particularly hazardous and dangerous work; to ensure primary education for all children; and to make a new law to stop all marriages for young people under the age of 18."

TEAM ENGLAND 2019

"Young people in the UK face a lot of barriers. We are often stereotyped – people associate us with gangs, drugs and violence. We are so much more than this. We are not asking for favours – we are demanding our rights. We demand from the government more funding for mental health awareness and support, educational programmes and opportunities, a level playing field for all young people, and a platform for our voice. Will you listen?"

TEAM ENGLAND 2018

"Our vision is for young people in London to have freedom of expression and to not be judged. Inspired by Street Child United, we hope to create a movement that could potentially impact the lives of young people around the world.

What are our demands? Well, we demand respect, we demand for people not only to hear our voices, but to take action. Within our local community we will be committed to finding a location for young people to feel they have a safe space to express themselves. We hope to work with local businesses and possibly schools to engage potential stakeholders. From the adults we ask only for the same patience and understanding we expect from each other.

We are strong, independent, resilient people determined to overcome any problem that stands in our way. We demand those of authority to utilise the power given to them by the people to actually make a change.

We ask them to help us both with money and publicity through the media. We must work together to create not just a brand, but a family. We, as passionate young people, demand acceptance and understanding, but it must start closer to home.

We must encourage each other to be the best version of ourselves before we can expect others to do the same."

Street Child United

"I am very glad to be here today as a street child who got the opportunity to come to Lord's to play cricket and to have my voice heard on behalf of other street children. We do not have gender equality and do not have access to education and healthcare. No child should work to earn for his or her food. We call on the government to act on these issues and to ensure that all children have these rights."

Forest Sunset by Team India North

TEAM INDIA SOUTH

"As street children we have no protection, and face many difficulties. We live on the streets because we have no place of our own. If we are asked to leave the streets, where will we go? We, street children from Chennai, voice our need for protection through the platform provided by Street Child United. We call on the government to respect the rights of street children and accept us as part of society. The government or police must not move us by force – this is totally against the rights of a child. To protect street children, basic necessities and facilities like clean bathrooms, toilets, quality water, clean food, medical facilities and quality education must be provided, for free, to all children who live on the streets. If you respect us, you will listen to us. If you listen to us, you will protect us."

"My name is Indu, I am from a non-profit organisation that supports street-connected children from the streets in India called Karunalaya.

We hope that the present and the future generations of children shall have a society which protects children from sexual abuse and violence. We hope there will be opportunities for children to go to school.

A child should never be a child labourer and should not face discrimination of gender, caste or race or any kind of language. A child should be protected from violence and have their rights respected.

Everyone should have a house to call a home, and that home should protect them from rain, sun, and be safe from fire.

Every street child should get a birth certificate, community certificate and all documents with no difficulty to them.

To display talents in sports, every street child should have a place to play. Street children should not be subjected to sexual violence or trafficked for abuse.

We hope that society shall understand and acknowledge that street children have good hearts, they are kind and want to display their talents. They are children like any other children in the world.

We are somebody and it is time to change our stories."

We Are Somebody

"We want to have our voices heard across the world. We want all children in Mauritius to be treated equally, whatever their background or ethnicity. We demand that our government provides homes for poor families as a right. We demand that our government provides formal education for children up to the age of 16, and also to provide healthcare for all children. Finally, we call on our government to raise awareness of issues around drug trafficking and addiction for children and child abuse. We believe that if you listen to our demands, we can have a better world for all street-connected children."

We Are Somebody

"I am here today representing all young people in Nepal. I am also here to demand that the rights of street children are guaranteed. I want all street children to have knowledge and skills and to be nurtured as equal citizens, so that they can contribute equally. Whilst living on the streets we had no access to proper clothing, very little to eat and physical and emotional abuse. Services like education and health were far from reach. To wear and eat just enough to survive, we had to walk in dangerous and hazardous conditions, which were not made for children. If you believe children should have rights, then we ask you to:

Ensure all children have access to equal and quality educational and health services, free of cost. Ensure all children are given legal identity (birth certificates) by their government and that these documents are easily accessible to everyone.

This Street Child Cricket World Cup event has brought us a step closer to achieving this."

"My name is Roshan, I was the Captain of Nepal in the Street Child World Cup. We hope that no child lives on the street, irrespective of caste, creed, religion. All kids, despite their situations, need food, shelter, education, health, family, love, and care.

Being a street child is not an identity - it is just an unfortunate situation. Society should respect us and support us. Governments should act like our parents, as we do not have them to care for us and help us create a better future. We are the future of the world, we are positive, we are kind, we are creative. Until a few months back we were termed as street children, we were attacked as criminals but today, we have an identity as national players. But today we are the change, we are the voice. To win the football game was our desire, but to win all the hearts is our aim."

We Are Somebody

Street Child United

"On the streets, children face physical, psychological and sexual violence. We are children, and we want the government to protect children and to give them social services including education, better healthcare and all the rights that other children have so that we can grow and develop. We would like this message to reach everybody — children, adults, police, community and the government."

"My name is Steria and I am from Tanzania. We hope that one day all children will be equal, which includes equal treatment, both boys and girls, education and healthcare provided without discrimination.

We want the government to provide areas for sport, so all young people have a safe space to play. Street children should be given opportunities to improve their situations and change their lives.

We are survivors, patient, talented, hard-working. We believe in ourselves. We are creative. We are smart. We accept and respect ourselves. We will be leaders and role models for other street children. We are somebody."

We Are Somebody

TEAM WEST INDIES

"We demand that our government hold parents accountable for failing to adequately care for and protect their children. Too often parents leave their children unattended, which can result in them being physically, emotionally, and sexually abused. We also call on the government to provide greater access to health, education and sporting facilities."

"My name is Sandra and I represented Mexico at the Street Child World Cup.

We demand equality for women, and for our goverment to believe in us as young women; to be supported and guided; to help us raise our voice.

We demand an end to the corruption and to have options and opportunities.

We are brave, we are capable, we represent all the children in Mexico, we are the future, we are somebody, and it's time to change our story."

"My name is Marina, I am from Kazakhstan.

We have a vision for the future. We hope there will be no wars, no discrimination, corruption, drugs, or abandoned children.

We demand our government will support young families and single mums, so that children won't be abandoned.

We demand education and healthcare become affordable for everyone in the world.

We also want children to have the opportunity to grow up as Sports and Arts Professionals.

If you want to change the world, you need to start talking about your problems and your requirements. We are somebody and it is time to change our story."

TEAM AMERICA

"My name is Juliana, I am from America.

Our vision is to be able to attain UNITY and EQUALITY for the human race that will open up a pathway for PEACE.

We demand gun reform, basic life needs for everyone and proper allocation of government resources. We demand education reform, equal treatment to ALL, and an end to separation of families through deportation.

We are the youth holding the world accountable for the right to LIFE, LIBERTY and the pursuit of HAPPINESS!

We are all somebody and it is time to change our story."

TEAM BOLIVIA

"My name is Denya, I am from the beautiful Bolivia.

Because of the Street Child World Cup we have understood that it is not only Bolivia that has problems, and that we share problems with many countries in the world.

We want the government to support us so that all street connected children have the right to identity and receive a birth certificate. Without this identification we cannot access education or healthcare. We demand respect for other cultures and for people to accept each other's values. We want to be heard. This will lead us to the equality of all nations.

We should remember that we are somebody and all of us deserve understanding, acceptance, and respect. Let us change our story."

We Are Somebody

TEAM PHILIPPINES

"I am Hendra from the islands of Philippines.

We demand to be treated as children or people, not as a piece of trash. We demand not to be abused by adults because we are young, strong and independent children.

We didn't expect to represent our country at a Street Child World Cup. Even though we are street children, we have learnt to value each other and take care of each other, because we believe that when we show we care, everybody wins."

Street Child United

"My name is Abdullah and I am from Pakistan. Alongside my team we represented Pakistan at the Street Child World Cup.

I was orphaned at the age of 2. Ijaz works in a brick factory, Nawaz works in crop fields; Ibrar works in cotton factories: we all face poverty and different problems. Despite our situations we are strong, we share our problems and help each other overcome them.

We are the children who have dreams for better futures, to make it for our families. We have learned so many things at the World Cup, experienced so many cultures and new experiences. We are taking so many new things back home that will make us better humans. We may lose games in football, but we will win the rights of street children in our country.

We are somebody and the future depends on us."

We Are Somebody

By Samantha Richards

So how do we survive?
How can we bring light into a world that seems only dark?
By sharing stories, by sharing experiences,
By sharing hope, and by inspiring one another.
Because when life goes astray,
There's one thing that will always stay the same:
Love.

We may speak different languages,
Might not seem compatible with the law of averages.
But we are human, we are people,
We should all have the possibility to be free and gleeful.
Just because we have all of these labels,
It doesn't mean our problems should be thrown under the table.

We all share ambition and dreams,
So why are we limited by what's in our genes?
For us, it's not just about the goals we score,
It's about our goals behind closed doors.
We have a voice and we demand it to be heard,
You have the choice: to be a sheep or lead the herd.

You are somebody,
I am somebody,
We are all somebody,

The future, OUR future depends on you.

Unique

By Agnes

The world we live in is black or white,
The best or the worst, the rich or the poor.

We live in fear of the unknown, scared to lose it all.
We try to fit in, hope to be accepted.
Behave out of character to receive attention, whether good or bad.
But enough is enough!

The world we should live in should be bright.
No divides between the good, beautiful,
Happy and the satisfied.
We should overcome our fears,
Live life to the fullest.

Proudly stand out: unique,
Bringing something new to the table.

Love, cherish one another,
Remember to do for others as we wish to be done to us.
After all, We Are All Somebody.

We Are All One

By Karina

I will be heard
I aspire to live in a world where freedom
And equality exist.

My race doesn't define me,
The income I make won't stop me,
Where there is aspiration, there is achievement.
We are all here together for the better.

In a world where class tries to determine my value,
I will not hold back,
I have no time for that,
I will move forward, not lose track.
Tengo orgullo Hispano.

The traditions I've been taught,
The obstacles that I've faced,
The life I've lived has made me who I am.
Tengo orgullo Hispano.

We are all equal,
Don't lose hope: one day, we'll be one.
In this world, we'll all belong,
Bonded by our love.

Our dear President, you have not loved us,
Your decision is foolish.

Change our society.
But how?
If you are the one who covered the mistakes,
Is it the wrongdoings of our society, or yours?

Mistakes do not change,
They cannot be covered,
I wish you, Sir, would come to terms with that.

The future, depends on you.

Respond

By Manty

All this killing is a death season
We were not prepared for you
There is not enough flesh in our kitchen to feed your hunger
We are restricted because of you
You cannot stay with us forever, Corona.

Don't think we want to live in lockdown
We will bring an end to the visits you make;
See hand washing become habit
We mourn for our closed churches and mosques,
But we will stay apart until you no longer visit us.

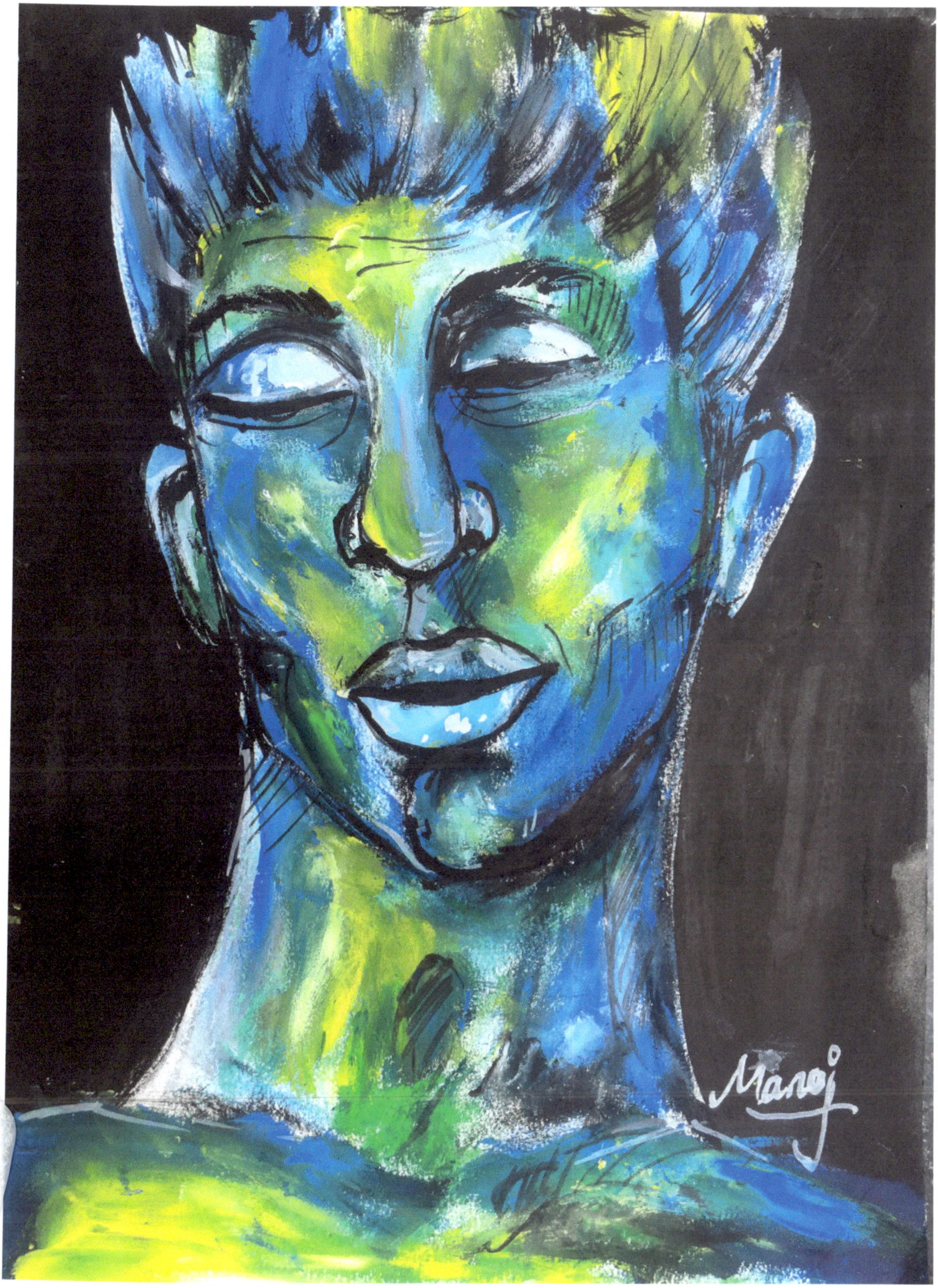
Manoj

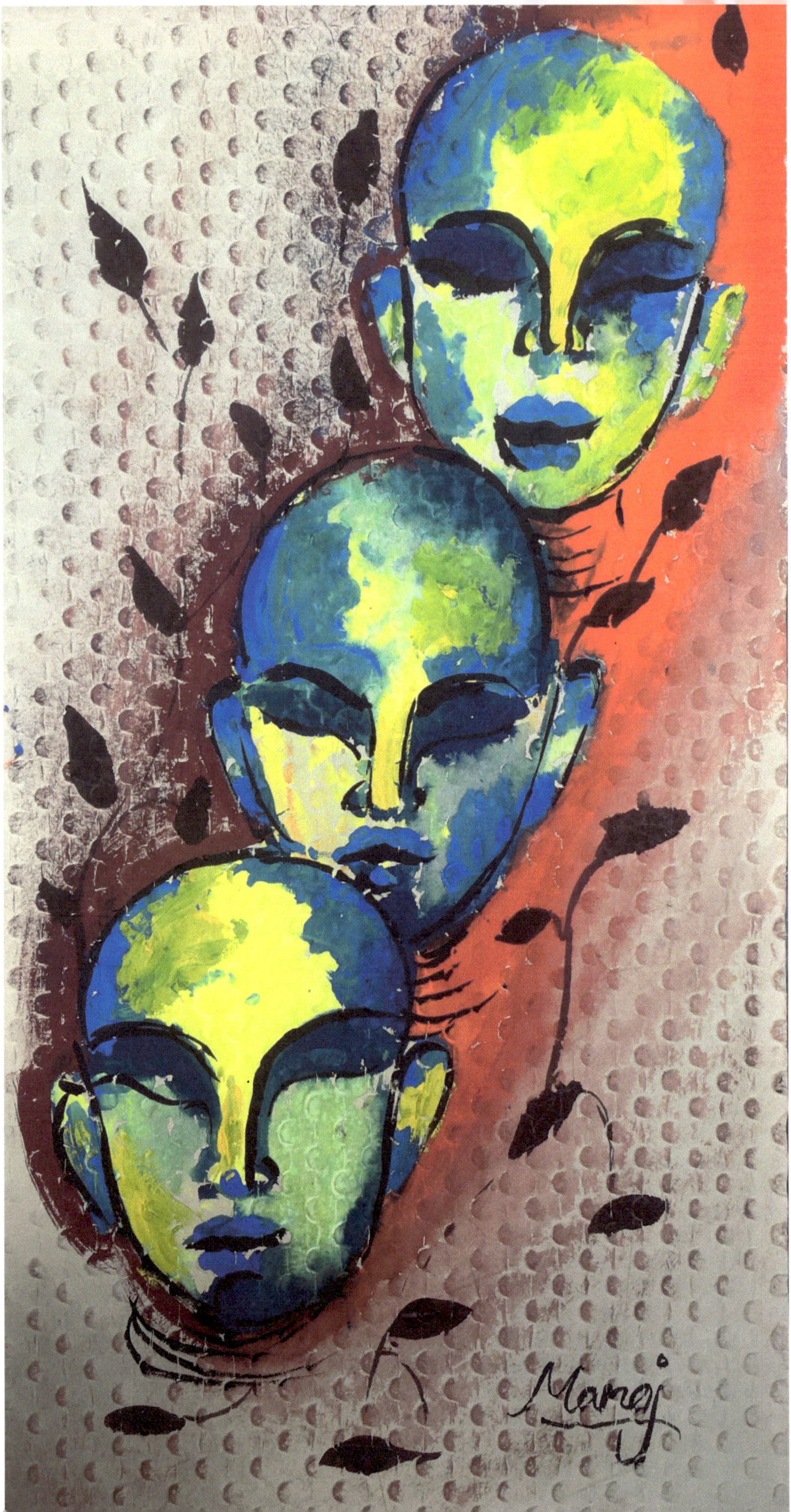
Manoj

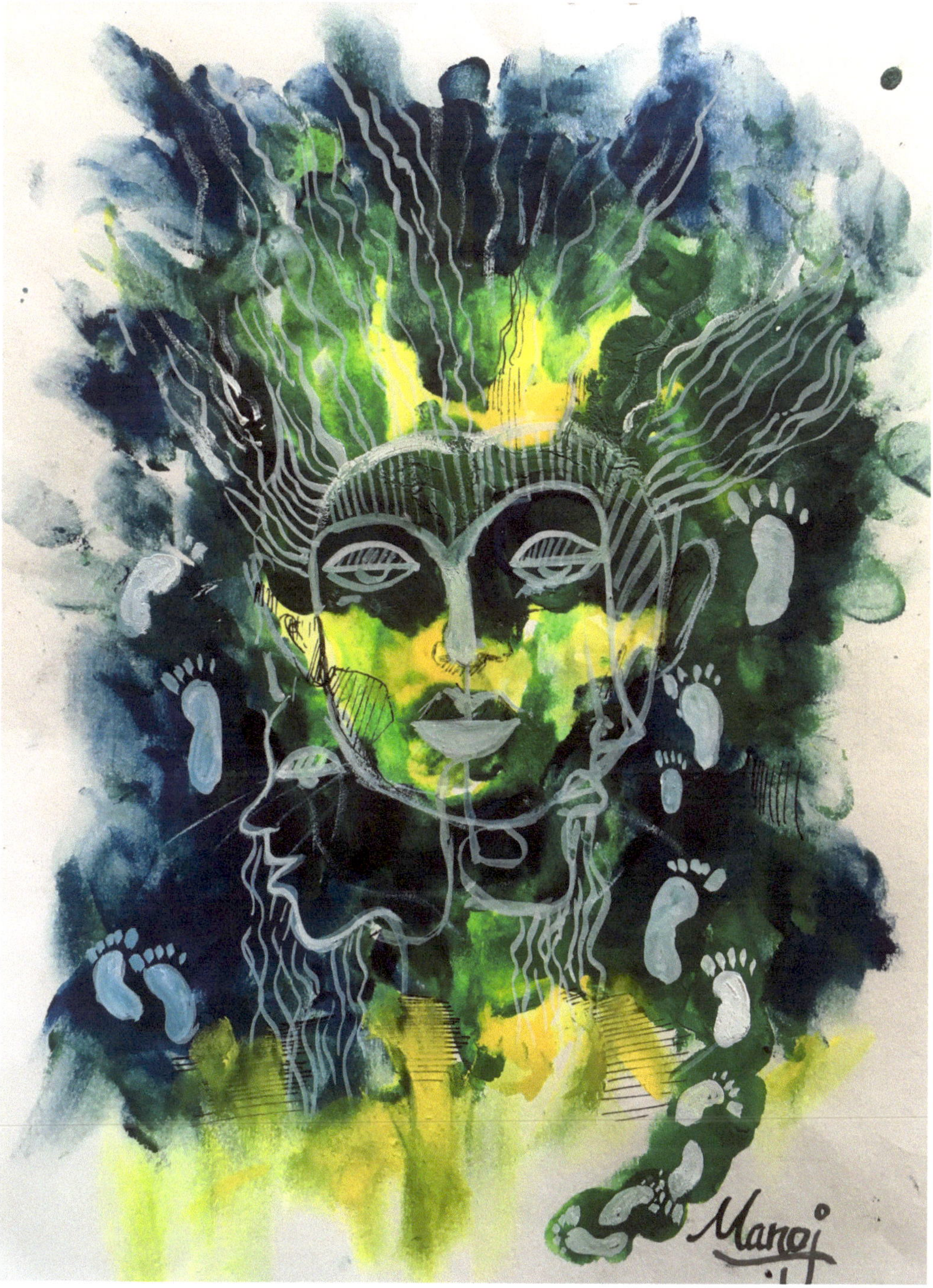
Manoj

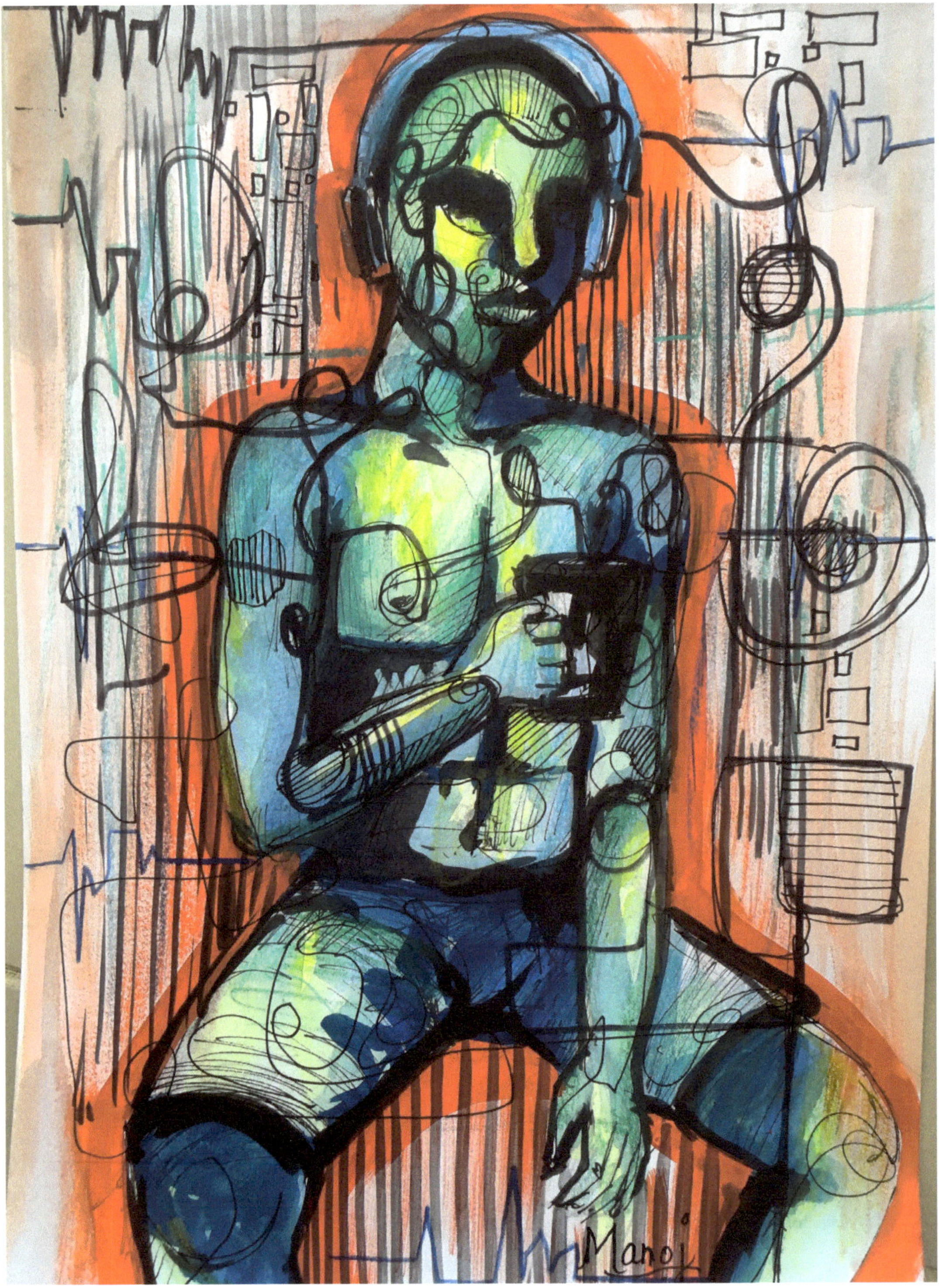
Manoj

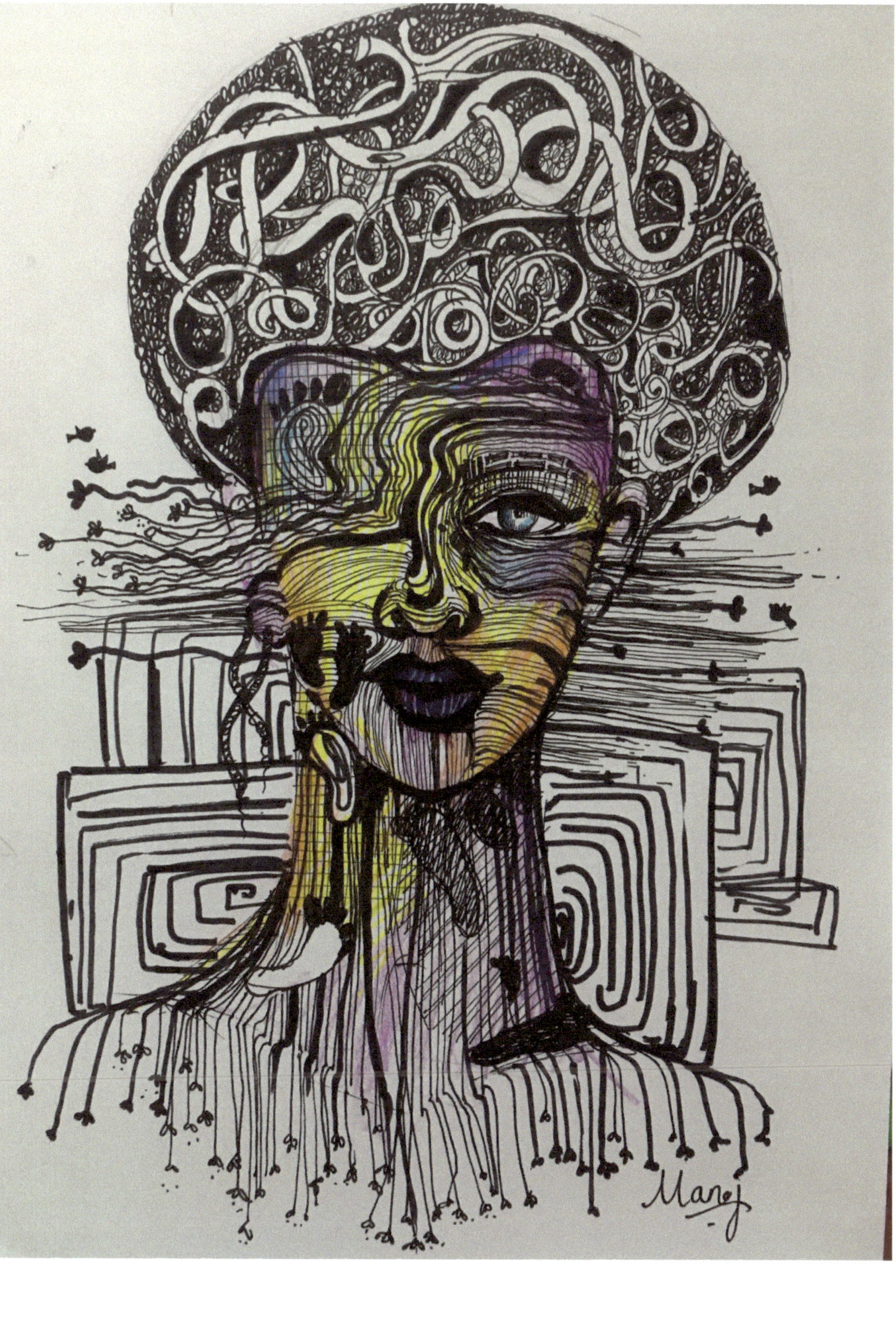
Manoj

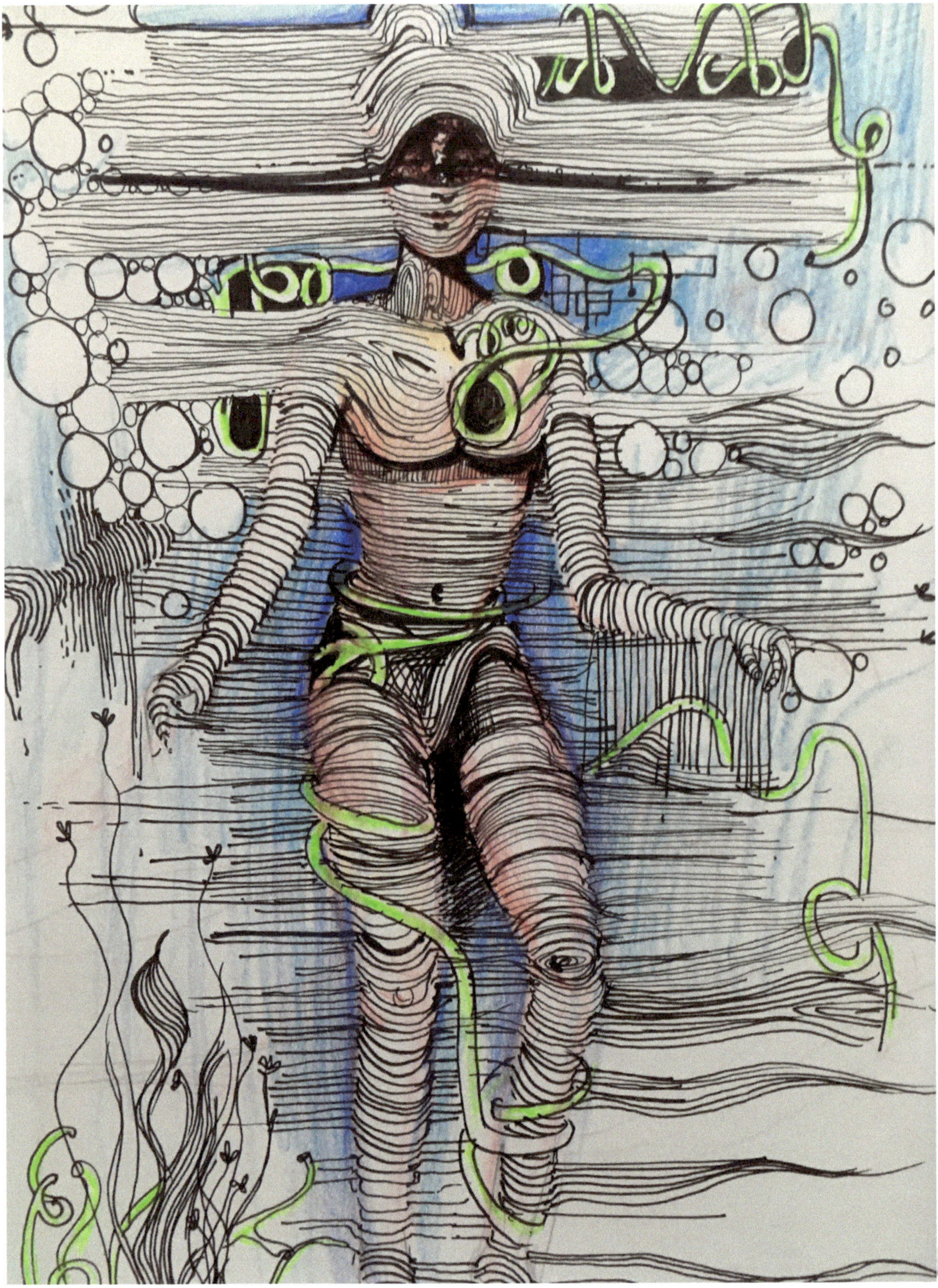

MANOJ MORE

Manoj More came to Salaam Baalak Trust Mumbai, an NGO for children in street situations, when he was 12 years old. He always had an interest in art. On the streets of Mumbai, when he did not have the means to draw, he would borrow extra pages and pencils from other children and sometimes even used the streets as his canvas.

Once at the shelter of the NGO, his basic requirements were fulfilled, and his potential in art recognized. He was encouraged to educate himself and draw as this also helped him express his feelings.

Today, as a confident young man of 23, he is pursuing his dream of becoming an architect, with full support from Salaam Baalak Trust.

Manoj hasn't given up his love for drawing, which he continues to pursue during his free time.

During the Covid lockdown he has been working at the shelter to encourage other younger boys to draw, guiding them with different techniques.

He has also just started teaching the basics of drawing on his YouTube channel "ABCD WITH MANOJ".

We Are All Family

By Samantha Richards

When people talk about love, I think about family:
People who have your back no matter what,
Who pick you up when you are down
And the people who you pick up too.

They are the people who make the good times last
And, equally, the people who stay through the bad.

They do not always share the same blood as you.
Or the same genetics, but you share the same heart,
Passion, values and hope.

You feel safe when you are with them, free to talk,
But most importantly, you feel free to be yourself.

When they are around you don't need to impress,
There is simply no need to be stressed.
Because they stop you from going west; getting depressed.
And they guide you to being your best.

I May Be

By Abdallah

I may be poor, but I Am Somebody.

I may be a child, but I Am Somebody.

I may be orphaned, or on the street, but I Am Somebody.

I may be small, but I Am Somebody.

I may make mistakes, but I Am Somebody.

My clothes are different, my face is different, my hair is different, but I Am Somebody.

I am black, brown, or white.

I speak different languages.

But I must be respected, and never rejected.

We Are All God's Creation.

Rise

By Sadock

Sunrise from the east.
My eyes facing the west.
I can feel the peace settle deeply in my chest.

Breakfast on my table,
I am starving no more.
Ready for my class sessions -
School bus at my door.

No booing in my class.
All we know is love and trust.
My teachers encourage me to pass,
I think my failures are my thirst.

The love in my family is amazing -
No fights at all.
Playing with my neighbours,
I take this chance to grow.

There are no drugs in my community,
Only hospitals for treatment.
Disability is not inability.
Nobody suffers from poverty.

Policemen are my friends;
They fight for children's rights.
No more children in gangs -
My future is bright.

Now I realise I am daydreaming.
I wish all this could be happening.
Like Martin Luther King,

I HAVE A DREAM.

A Girl

By Nisha

"Girl".
It's a simple word, but the world revolves around it.

When people aren't blessed with girls,
society suggests perhaps goddess *Laxmi* is keeping her blessings from them,
but when a girl is born, society exclaims in almost a pitiful tone,
"Oh, it's a girl!"

When she is born, sadness and disappointment is spread.
But "girl", she is also the one who takes away the sadness of the family,

From helping her mother with chores since childhood,
to taking full responsibility of running the household when grown-up,
Girl is the support system on which homes are built.
So why do people still say girls belong to their in-laws and are only
temporary guests in their own homes?

Leaving behind a house she made into a home for half her life,
she moves on, selflessly, to do the same for another house,
waiting to be filled with her love.
She accepts the new place happily, without looking back.

All this a girl does with a smile and with love,
only to hear more taunts and the same thing from society:
she doesn't belong.
"Oh, this is not her home, she belongs to her parents, that is where she came from."

Girl

She doesn't live her life for herself,
but for others.

Others who fail to provide her the simplest of things:
a sense of home, a sense of belonging.

Living day in and day out, with the will to do whatever it takes to keep
the household going…
One day, she gives up.

She asks, while she leaves this harsh world behind,
"Why is it, that men can get away with anything but
if a Girl makes even one slight mistake,
all her efforts are suddenly forgotten,
and the mistake becomes the only thing that defines her?
Why is that?" she asks.

A Girl is stepped over, every step; put down but never lifted up.
Is it only me that's unable to see the changes people talk of?
Where is the equality that is being talked about?

We easily point out that a Girl's life is full of struggles,
but can we not do something to ease them?
For her happiness, can we not even let her know,
"It is your life, you must live it without any restrictions!
You are a girl, yes. But you hold the right to live your life happily."

We Are United

By Farijal

We street-connected children of Kenya are:

Strong,

Courageous,

Bright and intelligent,

United and supporting each other.

We never give up or lose hope for a better life,

And we believe in ourselves.

We demand that the government of Kenya stops rounding up street children

And putting them in prison.

We also demand that all 12 rehabilitation schools across the country are

Transformed into education and sports academies.

Because we are somebody. And it is time to change.

Hello, COVID-19

By Razib

Hello, COVID-19.

We do not know where the end to your tyranny will be,
every day you terminate many lives, including innocent street children.

We are terrified of you.
You changed shaking hands into waving hands.
We think you might be hungry.
You have killed nearly two million lives all over the world.
If you are still hungry for more innocent souls,
then go to them who are more dangerous than you.

You take from the rich,
And extract from the poor.
Does the world forget about us?
The ones who sleep on the floor.

We do not want to suffer your atrocities.
You forced us to stay at home.
You took the joy of innocent street-children.
This is just because of your idiocy.
You have no mercy on us.

Please go away from us.
We do not want to suffer you anymore.
I anticipate your forgiveness if I have erred in writing to you COVID-19.
Please do not come to us.

Why?

By Safiyyah

Why do people discriminate against others,
Based on their beliefs and skin colour?
They feel the need to antagonise them,
Regardless of whether they're children or adults.

It's devasting to feel racism everywhere:
One racist word can make your heart tear.
People feel the need to taunt other people,
Firing derogatory words to mark them less equal.

Hatred and racism is not something you are born with.
Rather, it is a disease that people give
To younger generations, so they feel it's okay
To hate people based on difference every day.

When it comes down to it, we're all just one human race
And there is no one superior, in any case.
Black, brown or white – you're no less of a human being
Why do people hate others based on colours they're seeing?

Why can't the world come together in peace
And all racism, hatred and war be ceased?
At the end of the day, we're just flesh and bones,
Regardless of our beliefs; the colour of our skin.

Speak the truth

By Aman Bharti

Speak the truth:
Take the pain and use the pen.

Poverty; hunger chews children,
I ask you:
Sing the song of those in hunger,
Take the pain and use the pen.

Our heartless leader enjoys bread,
Whilst masses die in labour:
Take the pain and use the pen.

The world is listening, so, are you singing?
Change the world, for your siblings.

Play the music of your own,

Speak the truth or don't speak at all:
Take the pain and use the pen.

Soul of the Street

By Taofeek

Up above the ground you will find birds' nests.
Here and there on the floor you will find rats' houses.
But they have their rooms on the street.
Like a ship lost in the middle of the ocean,
Tossed in a mighty storm with great eruption,
That is how their souls are, from now 'till the next generation.
As you slept on a soft foam mattress,
Wrapping yourself with a warm blanket,
That shielded you from harshness of cold in the night,
They enjoyed the roughness of wood and nylon.
Who cares what they are sleeping on!

At the same time, they are in a mighty war with mosquitos.
Uncomfortable, but they are holding on.
Thank God it's morning! You wake up.
Wash your teeth, take your bath, you are freshening up.
With the sweetness of a delicious meal, your mouth is filled up,
Full of joy, well-equipped, you can't mess up.
For them, morning has nothing to show for itself,
No food, no water; mouths parched.
Picking and eating from what you have condemned,
Not even to be dog food.
Day after day, insecurity and hunger are their greatest threats.
But with nothing to fight, they must enjoy them as joy-givers.
Look at them, what are your thoughts?
Have they not suffered a lot?

But you still nail them with the reason:
They found themselves on the street!

They should be treated with care in our country.
Help them not to be a threat.
SOULS OF THE STREET
Where is your helper?

From the streets, to home

By Ugochukw

My mother died when I was eleven.

I never knew my father.

Nobody cared for me.

I started picking scrap to sell, so I could eat.

I lived alone.

I slept in waste bins.

Big boys stole my money.

Each day, I would beg to eat.

Street life was not easy.

But a good Samaritan helped,

And brought me to Child Life Line.

I'm back in school.

I have a home.

COVID-19

By Mohammed Koroma

Oh, what is this thing called COVID-19
Which has put the whole world on hold?
I've heard that crowds no longer gather together,
This unknown threat has ruined our peace,
The peace of so many at once, like never before.
I am sure millions are infected,
some have found a different kind of peace in death.
Like HIV and AIDs, for now, it resists vaccine
The world's scientists say we are facing great challenges.
It spreads like the bush fire in the harmattan seasons.

The World Health Organization is pouring money
BBC, CNN, our local press talk of nothing else
Do you think it only comes for the white? No.
Many black people are also victims.
Follow the precautions, free us from its grip.
Stop the arguments, the questions of its source
Stop political manoeuvres, which risk exposing others
Stop the lies on social media, we must be strong.

We have lockdown, curfew and hand washing
Social distancing and instructions to wear masks
The whole world is in unison
Without vaccines, it's about human commitment
It wants to destroy us, and all our economic developments
Many are dead, jobless, so focus
You have commitments you must uphold.

Hope for the future
By Opeyemi

Sorrow brings pain,

living with no home, no help.

Street life is like a great war,

focus and determination help you survive,

if you are lucky and make no mistakes.

Trying times of heartache and pain.

Hope and dreams shatter,

prayers seem to be in vain.

With hope and peace diminishing,

the heart has no definitive song.

The struggle seems so long.

Yet there is hope for the future,

why should we despair?

God will make the ultimate decision.

He mourns and counts every tear,

hears and reviews every prayer.

Street Trouble

By Jimoh

My mother left my father and carried my small brother away.
My father died of AIDS within a year.
My father's family took us in but separated us.
They used me as a house boy.
At the market was a river, and some boys swimming.
I joined them and met a boy.

He asked, "Are you a street boy?"
"No, I came to sell pure water", I said.
"Are you a street boy?"
"Yes", he said; we became friends.

He wanted to go to Lagos.
I asked him if helpers were there.
He said "yes", so I followed.
As we reached Lagos, we bought food.
He held what was left of our money.
We stood up to go under the bridge.
I looked back; he wasn't there.

I went to sleep and woke to people running.
The Task Force were chasing us.
I ran into broken bottles.
I walked and begged for money, food and help,
In the middle of the night.
Wherever I stopped, the police came along to pick up street boys.
I ran away again.

They left me and I found a way to sleep.

I heard the sounds of gun shots, saw the older boys running.

They also chased me and took my money.

This is street life, street trouble!

Opposite: Artwork by Thamizharasi, India.

Street Child United

Coronavirus dans les rues

Par Ange

Le coronavirus nous empêche d'être heureux, car dangereux

Parmi les milles et une astuces, que nous donne Quitus, le combat peut se gagner tel Spartacus

Sécurité sociale, médicament, confinement. Cette maladie nous plonge dans une sorte d'asservissement.

Se protéger ? Mais comment ? En se lavant les mains avec de l'eau propre et du savon. En se tenant à bonne distance, les uns des autres et même de ceux que nous aimons.

Et vous mesdames et messieurs du gouvernement, prenez en considération que les enfants de la rue sont plus exposés

Nous vous prions d'agir, ne négligez pas la création des foyers d'accueil aux mesures d'hygiène convenable afin que le confinement soit respecté

Enfants de la rue en difficulté, nous gardons espoir

Coronavirus in the Streets

By Ange

The coronavirus brings danger; prevents us from being happy…

To find liberation, we need a thousand and one tricks

Then we can win this fight like Spartacus.

Social security, medication, lockdown,

This disease has resulted in a kind of bondage…

Protect yourself? But how?

By washing your hands with clean water and soap.

By keeping a safe distance from even those we love.

How can we do that? Ladies and gentlemen

of the government, take into account

Us street children: we urge you to act

Not to neglect the creation of shelters

With proper hygiene measures

And keep the virus contained

These are difficult times for street children

But we hope.

The Story of a Street Child

By Gladys

I am a child like any other. I live on the street.
Dangerous, harsh, stinking,
my home is the unfriendly, violent street.
My full name is 'street child'.
The world is my street and the street is my world.
I was born to use the gifts and talents within me.
I would like to grow up like other children, surrounded by love and care.

My battle with fate seems unending, the street
holds me back from my noble destiny
I strive to survive along with despairing others.
Each day I try to make the street my home
But, on the street, I am despised
I am unprotected from the weather,
panic-stricken by the thought
of sicknesses, ailments, illnesses.

On the street I am scorned, blamed, used and abused.
Except by those who share my destiny -
every other person turns away.
When needed, I am a human 'donkey'
a 'beast of burden' on the street, perhaps.

Who is looking at my face to see my brokenness?
Who is looking at my dirty, tattered ware?
Who is looking at my cracked feet?

Who is looking at my open wounds?
I am wounded time and time again but few care.

I am unjustly treated by the people for whom I carry a baby
and a pan to labour.
My little earnings are survival for family.
When I feel annoyed with those who owe me livelihood,
I am overwhelmed by pity at their helplessness,
their hunger, their daily toil for so little.

I am always asking myself:
How do I understand my street world?
Where did I go wrong, what did I do?
Whose fault is it I'm here, and
will anybody help me?

Keep quiet street child!
Keep quiet kayayo!
Keep quiet 'beast of burden' on the street
Does anyone care?

I am a child like any other.

Precautions

By Sheku

Health workers know about every deadly disease
But they have no vaccine for Covid-19
This airborne disease, spreading faster by the day
All they have is precautions:
Don't touch your nose, mouth, eyes, wash your hands in case you do
Avoid overcrowding, don't break quarantine
Every suspect should report themselves and call 117
Soap, water, sanitizers are your weapons,
Follow lockdown and curfew, it strengthens the fight
Or by-laws if they are needed, advise your friends
And your family; give them credit and support
Avoid social media where Corona seems to rule
If you do all of this, you *might* keep your job,
You might keep your life.

Implications

By Alhaji

All churches and mosques are closed
Christians and Muslims cannot gather, they watch.
Pastors and Imams give no sermons,
Schools are closed, the virus moves in on us
Teachers wonder about students' futures
Parents and guardians fear this reckoning.

No games are played, no sport can be watched
Cinemas, public events, everything is cancelled
The world is being destroyed,
Standards of living
Drop
As the virus ascends.

Restrictions and job losses increase:
This virus levels all prejudice;
Leaves analysts and scientists in the dark.

Destruction

By Amanita

You close churches and mosques
Shut schools; make children stay at home
Sport cannot be played or watched by your decree
The world economy is already stranded
Family, love, friendships wait for you to end
And though our lives are different in comfort,
You kill black and white the same
To you, there is no difference
Between the rich and the poor
But we will end your time in this world
We will do what we can, put in the effort
of that you can be sure.

COVID-19, We Shall Threaten You
By Amadu

Get out of my country and allow us to grow

Get out of this place before the cock crows

Get out of my nation; you will never rule us

How dare you get in the way of our plans?

How dare you bring us hardship?

How dare you stop our comfort?

Never get in the way of our worship again

Never think you are powerful, because we have more

Soon we will start hammering down on you like the August rains

The army and the police will keep the rules in place until you're gone

The hand washing, the face masks, the distancing until you're gone

This is our country, you must leave

Very soon, our sports will resume

You will see our victory

Very soon, churches and mosques will return

You will see our victory

Very soon, schools will be full again

And we will celebrate our victory.

Corona, Return To Your Harbour

By Margret

Out of Ebola I escaped
Victory was mine, but death spilled
Holding a thousand pains, my eyes
saw beds of sandstone; watched as love died.

Grief held me ransom, no therapy could help
No tears could bring back laughter
Everything that lives, even the beautiful,
can be ambushed by death.
No single *gugu* in this world is safe.

Corona treats us just as badly as Ebola
I cherish the memory of beautiful souls
coming home, when Corona could have let them go.
Stubborn like a teenager, she has no respect for age
But if thou embrace face masks
Avoid crowds, wash hands constantly
I know cowardly Corona will return to her harbour
Slowly, bit by bit, her hunger will cease.

Many healthy people are in lockdown, distraught
When will you leave us, make the pandemic a memory?
Besieged, Nigrus Nigras as worshippers no longer express their faith
Greatly afraid like children and kongoli, of the inevitable death
Corona has power like the God of the creation story
But Corona uses it like a missile to kill even though we plead
For forgiveness, burning like Sodom and Gomorrah.

We need to remember the past to overcome this threat

As our future unfolds, Corona spreads like impiety

Gambling with our economy and silencing our temple

Corona holds fake victory, runs across the garden, while we struggle.

Cowardly Corona return to your harbour

my father is coming for us.

A Tale of the Sitting Room

By Musa, Juma, Rafeal, Gasta, Muzafaru, Paul, Omal, Mohammed, Shafik, Charles, Yasini, Owen, Ashraf, Alpha, Yusuf, Moses, Harunah, Bakali, Mutwalibi, Peter, Yasini, Brian, and Phillip

Walking bare-footed, in tattered clothes,
from railway stations to bus stations,
from big markets to slums,
on pavements through the hustle and bustle of the city
telling stories, painfully and shamefully
of how they ended up on the streets.

"Abusive mothers"
"Sexually exploitative families"
"I fled to be free, as the pain was too much to bear"

Escaping from poverty, shoulder to shoulder
Now lonely walking on the streets of the unknown.

"We do sniff 'mafuta', it keeps us warm in the cold"
"When I am lonely, I sniff it more"
"When I am with my friends, they give me more"
"When you don't sniff it, you are a misfit"
"I can't help but go on"

With friends you are happy in different ways
Without them, you are hungry for days
If you don't share what you have with me
I won't share with you, that's how it works.

We sleep in a group
If you sleep alone, you are sexual prey
If you sleep too deeply, your money gets taken
The gangs of the night scare us so much
The leaders and their thugs often look for us
We are scared, whereas they have an aura about them.

We are not lazy, maybe a bit crazy
but we are always busy working
collecting scraps and plastics to make money.
Playing football is our way of freeing our minds
Music and dance curb our miseries.

People keep their distance from us, disregard us
but there is a rainbow beyond the rain.
We want to be an inspiration, to make a mark beyond
to contribute to the change and see a better world
All this seems so strange, but I know what we can be
if only you stand with us.

Is It Right?

By Tamizharasi

At the age of bearing schoolbags, is it right
To make me bear a bag of stones?

Should I have to hold tea glasses,
Instead of holding a pen in my hand?

Is it right for me to do manual labour,
At an age for playing happily?

Is it right to confine children like me into the kitchen?
Or to treat children like me as a labourer?

Thank You

By Samantha Richards

Thank you,
A simple gesture it may seem,
Thank you,
For your help and support in this team.

We have projected our voices,
Sky Sports, and the BBC,
Sometimes I think I'm dreaming,
This is so crazy!

Thinking about our stories,
My heart begins to hurt,
Thinking about what we have been through,
To the age we have to work.

A chance was taken on me,
A chance was taken on the 75 other teams,
Governments, and the authorities,
Are finally starting to listen to the minority.

So, thank you,
For being brave.
Thank you for being true.
There is honestly no one else,
Quite like you!

We Are Somebody

About Street Child United

Street Child United is a UK-based charity with a unique and proven model for delivering social impact – using the power of sport to provide a global platform for street children to be seen and their voices heard. Ahead of the world's biggest sporting competitions, we organise international sports events for street children to change the way young people like them are seen and treated across the globe.

Our ten-day events see street-connected young people from around the world come together to partake in a football or cricket tournament; a festival of arts; and advocate for their rights and protection through our UN-style congress and General Assembly. Ahead of the FIFA and ICC World Cups, the SCWC will give the most vulnerable children from across the globe the chance to represent their country and tell the world that they are somebody.

Samantha is a Street Child United Young Leader. All of our Young Leaders are former participants from Street Child World Cups, who are supported with personalised development plans. Our Change10 Programme is a year-long programme which includes a 20 week online course designed to upskill our Young Leaders around the world. An individual support and mentorship programme for each young person ensures we continue to guide our young people as they embark on higher education or further their career. Our Young Leaders are powerful and influential, and we work to ensure that they are supported to become leaders in their communities and agents of change.

Social Media:

@StreetChildUtd (Twitter)

@streetchildutd (Instagram)

@streetchildunited (Facebook)

www.streetchildunited.org

About Fly on the Wall Press

A publisher with a conscience.
Publishing high quality anthologies on pressing issues, chapbooks and poetry products, from exceptional poets around the globe.
Founded in 2018 by founding editor, Isabelle Kenyon.

Other publications:

Please Hear What I'm Not Saying
(February 2018. Anthology, profits to Mind.)

Persona Non Grata
(October 2018. Anthology, profits to Shelter and Crisis Aid UK.)

Bad Mommy / Stay Mommy by Elisabeth Horan
(May 2019. Chapbook.)

The Woman With An Owl Tattoo by Anne Walsh Donnelly
(May 2019. Chapbook.)

the sea refuses no river by Bethany Rivers
(June 2019. Chapbook.)

White Light White Peak by Simon Corble
(July 2019. Artist's Book.)

Second Life by Karl Tearney
(July 2019. Full collection)

The Dogs of Humanity by Colin Dardis
(August 2019. Chapbook.)

Small Press Publishing: The Dos and Don'ts by Isabelle Kenyon
(January 2020. Non-Fiction.)

Alcoholic Betty by Elisabeth Horan
(February 2020. Chapbook.)

Awakening by Sam Love
(March 2020. Chapbook.)

Grenade Genie by Tom McColl
(April 2020. Full Collection.)

House of Weeds by Amy Kean and Jack Wallington
(May 2020. Full Collection.)

No Home In This World by Kevin Crowe
(June 2020. Short Stories.)

How To Make Curry Goat by Louise McStravick
(July 2020. Full Collection.)

The Goddess of Macau by Graeme Hall
(August 2020. Short Stories.)

The Prettyboys of Gangster Town by Martin Grey
(September 2020. Chapbook.)

The Sound of the Earth Singing to Herself by Ricky Ray
(October 2020. Chapbook.)

Inherent by Lucia Orellana Damacela
(November 2020. Chapbook.)

Medusa Retold by Sarah Wallis
(December 2020. Chapbook.)

Social Media:
@fly_press (Twitter)
@flyonthewall_poetry (Instagram)
@flyonthewallpress (Facebook)
www.flyonthewallpress.co.uk

We Are Somebody